HighSchool
Host Club
™

Vol. 4
Bisco Hatori

Ouran High School

Host Club™

Vol. 4

CONTENTS

CAST

HARUHI FUJIOKA ‹1-A›
A SCHOLARSHIP STUDENT WITH A BLUNT PERSONALITY.
THE CLUB'S CUSTOMERS ARE UNAWARE THAT SHE IS A GIRL. ♥

TAMAKI SUOH ‹2-A›
HOST CLUB PRESIDENT AND
SUPPOSEDLY THE MOST REQUESTED
HOST. SOMEWHAT NARCISSISTIC AND
SLIGHTLY DENSE.

KYOYA OHTORI ‹2-A›
HOST CLUB VICE PRESIDENT. A COOL STRATEGIST.
WHAT IS HE THINKING BEHIND THAT SMILE?

HIKARU HITACHIIN ‹1-A›
EASYGOING AND LIVES BY THE
PHILOSOPHY OF "OTHERS = TOYS."
THE OLDEST OF THE TWINS. VIRGO.

KAORU HITACHIIN ‹1-A›
HANDSOME HOMOSEXUAL + FORBIDDEN LOVE BETWEEN
RELATIVES + SYMMETRY IS HIS NICHE. VIRGO.

MITSUKUNI HANINOZUKA ‹3-A›
GOES BY THE NICKNAME "HUNNY."
ALWAYS HAS HIS TOY BUNNY.

TAKASHI MORINOZUKA ‹3-A›
GOES BY THE NICKNAME "MORI." A MEMBER OF THE
KENDO CLUB. HE QUIETLY WAITS UPON HUNNY.

STORY

THIS STORY TAKES PLACE AT OURAN INSTITUTE, AN ULTRA-
EXCLUSIVE PRIVATE HIGH SCHOOL. HARUHI, A SCHOLARSHIP STUDENT
OF NO LINEAGE OR WEALTH, WANDERS INTO MUSIC ROOM 3, WHERE
SHE ENCOUNTERS ALL SIX HANDSOME MEN OF THE HOST CLUB.
ALTHOUGH UNINTERESTED IN THEM, HARUHI MANAGES TO KNOCK
OVER A VASE (PRICE TAG: $80,000!) AND, TO REPAY THE DEBT, IS
OBLIGED TO BECOME A CLUB MEMBER. ▶LATER, HAVING TAKEN AN
INTEREST IN THE WAYS OF THE COMMON FOLK, TAMAKI AND THE
OTHERS VISIT HARUHI'S HOME. UNFORTUNATELY, WHEN TAMAKI AND
HARUHI ARE ALONE TOGETHER, TAMAKI MANAGES TO KNOCK OVER
HARUHI, JUST IN TIME FOR HARUHI'S DAD TO COME HOME AND
WITNESS THE SCENE...

THE DAUGHTER IS SPLAYED OUT ON THE FLOOR (OR SO IT SEEMS).

THE STRANGER IS THE ONE WHO SPLAYED HER (OR SO IT SEEMS).

THE FATHER RETURNS UNEXPECTEDLY. (HE WORKS AT A TRANNY BAR.)

RYOJI FUJIOKA (AGE 35)

TAMAKI INSTANTLY GRASPS THE ENTIRETY OF THE SITUATION.

5

1

HELLO, EVERYONE!
THIS IS HATORI! IT'S
VOLUME 4 OF HOST CLUB!!

HOW CAN I SAY THIS...
FOR THIS VOLUME, I FELT
AN UNPRECEDENTED
SENSE OF URGENCY, IN
TIME AND IN SOME OTHER
MATTERS. ♪ I MEAN, I
HAVE THE DISTINCT
FEELING THAT I RAN
SMACK INTO ONE OF THE
WALLS I NEED TO CLIMB
OVER, IF I AM TO
CONTINUE TO DRAW
MANGA. ♪♪

I WANT TO APOLOGIZE
FOR A LOT OF THINGS,
LIKE THE ROUGHNESS OF
THE DRAWINGS--MY GOAL
THIS TIME WAS JUST TO
"FINISH IT INSTEAD OF
REDOING IT." AS LONG AS
TIME PERMITS, I PLAN ON
DRAWING RELENTLESSLY,
SO PLEASE CHEER ME ON.

THE OBJECT OF THE
COLUMNS IN VOLUME 4
IS THE ANNOUNCEMENT
OF THE RESULTS FOR THE
"HOST CLUB MEMBERS
OFFICIAL BIRTHDAY
DETERMINATION EVENT"
IN *LALA* MAGAZINE, AND
TO TALK A LITTLE ABOUT
THE CHARACTERS. SO,
LET'S MOVE ON TO THE
NEXT COLUMN.
← GO!!

THERE ARE COLUMNS IN
ODD PLACES THIS TIME, SO
PLEASE PAY ATTENTION!

HARUHI, AGE 9

ER... RROTS, OTA- TOES...

MY DAUGHTER LOST HER MOTHER AT A VERY YOUNG AGE.

AND SHE NOT ONLY TOOK CARE OF THE CHORES AROUND THE HOUSE BUT THE SHOPPING TOO.

I WONDERED IF SHE WAS HURTING...

AH. I SEE.

IN A PLACE LIKE THIS, IT'S IMPOSSIBLE NOT TO NOTICE.

CREEP CREEP

ATTA GIRL, HARUHI!!

YEAH...

SIGH

I GUESS IT WAS JUST FATHERLY CONCERN

...SO I COULDN'T HELP FOLLOWING HER IN SECRET.

FATHER, AGE 29. A FLEDGLING CROSS-DRESSER. HIS MAKEUP IS STILL THIN.

HE HASN'T CHANGED AT ALL.

THOSE

PITIFUL! HA HA HA HA HA

BECAUSE YOU DON'T HAVE A MOM, YOUR DAD IS TAKING HER PLACE, RIGHT?

HA HA HA!

CLASSMATE

HEY!

THERE'S HARUHI!!

YOU-- BRATS!!

WHY ARE YOU ALONE? YOUR GAY DAD ISN'T WITH YOU?

ARGH!

NOT REALLY. IT'S NOT PITIFUL.

B-DMP

ER, LET'S SEE WHAT'S OVER THERE.

IT'S CALLED AN "INNATE PREFERENCE."

IT'S MY DAD'S HOBBY.

ZWIP

DO YOU WANT TO HOLD THE BASKET AGAIN?

EXPOSED

WHAT'RE YOU DOING, DAD?

TRUM TRUM

Y-YEAH?

UH.

YES!! I MISSED HOLDING THE BASKET.

PAPA SURE LOVES HOLDING THAT BASKET!!

WHAT AN EXCUSE...

NOT KIDDING!!

AH HA HA HA HA HA

I'VE GOTTEN USED TO IT.

HARUHI...

I DON'T KNOW IF I SHOULD BE HAPPY OR SAD.

HEY, TAMAKI!! PLEASE STOP! WE'RE IN A SUPER-MARKET!!

WINTER LIMITED

BUT SOMEDAY...

...IF THAT GIRL...

...WANTS TO BE WITH SOMEONE ELSE, WITH ALL HER HEART...

HARUHI!! MEAT, PLEASE!!

IS THIS A HOMEMADE MEAL?

OKAY, OKAY.

YUMMY, HUH?

↑
THEY WOUND UP USING A KOTATSU TABLE.

COMMON FOLK'S MEAT!!

WOW, THIS MEAT IS DOGGONE TOUGH.

I WANT... MEAT...

YAY!

HA HA HA. MAKE SURE TO SAVOR IT.

HERE.

THERE'S PLENTY OF CHINESE CABBAGE.

ARGH!

THE VERY THOUGHT IRRITATES ME.

I'M GOING TO BULLY HIM TO DEATH.

FLURP FLUP

EPISODE 14

VALENTINE'S DAY.
THE FESTIVAL MOST DEAR
TO ANY YOUNG LADY.

AND THE
EXTRAORDI-
NARILY
WEALTHY
YOUNG LADIES
OF OURAN
ARE NO
EXCEPTION.

St. Valentine's Day

February 14th

THEIR
CONVERSATION
TURNS TO
WHAT TRINKETS
TO BESTOW ON
THE MEN IN
THEIR HEARTS.

Music Room 3

THERE IS
ANOTHER,
THOUGH...

MOUSSE?
BON-
BONS?

HUNNY! ♡
WHAT KIND
OF CHOCO-
LATE WOULD
YOU LIKE
THIS YEAR?

...WHO WAS
DYING FOR
THAT DAY TO
ARRIVE.

WHAT
COLOR
RIBBON?

FEB. 10

FOUR DAYS UNTIL
VALENTINE'S DAY!

HUNNY!

I love chocolate and all you too. ♡

I'd be happy with any. ♡

EEEEEEE!♡

MITSUKUNI HANINOZUKA (AGE 17). THIRD-YEAR AT OURAN PRIVATE INSTITUTE. MEMBER OF THE HOST CLUB.

HEIGHT ☆ 4' 11"

PISCES, BLOOD TYPE AB

BUN-BUN

EXCELLENT ☆ MATH STUDENT

HIS FAVORITE THINGS ARE CAKES, CHOC- OLATES, AND BUN-BUN.

AND THE FLOWER GARDEN.

EXCELS AT ☆ BUNNY KICKS, ETC.

HIS LOVELINESS IS INVINCIBLE.

THE PRETERNATURAL SUGAR ☆ BOY (OUTDATED JIVE) OF OURAN. IN A PAST LIFE, WAS HE RABBIT OR BEE?

HUNNY FLOWERS ↓

HUNNY AND HIS HAPPY FRIENDS

HIKARU KAORU

TAMAKI

TAKASHI

KYOYA

HARUHI

ME!

THE SCENE WAS SIMPLY TOO EXCITING FOR SOME GIRLS.

TAMAKI...

AH, YES.

UNDER-
STOOD.

CAVITY

KK

PO

...

BOOM!!!

KRAKK

Waah

THUS BEGAN...

DEAR CUSTOMERS:
THE HOST CLUB WILL NOT BE PARTICIPATING IN VALENTINE'S DAY.

...HUNNY'S DAYS OF MISERY.

DONG DONG
DONG DONG

GOOD MORNING.

FEB. 11

PUF FY

※ DAYS WITHOUT SWEETS: 1

CHATTER

IT MUST BE REALLY HARD ON HUNNY.

I KNOW I SHOULDN'T SAY THIS, BUT HE LOOKS LIKE...

AW, I FEEL SO SORRY FOR HUNNY.

I'VE HEARD THE HOST CLUB ISN'T PARTICI- PATING IN VALENTINE'S DAY.

...A BUNNY RABBIT!

EEEEE!

LOVELY!

THAT'S NOT IT. SHOW ME.

I can carry it myself.

MITSU- KUNI, YOUR BAG...

Th...

They're only for looking.

I wasn't going to eat them.

REALLY.

...

KLIK

CHOCO- LATES

CANDIES

GUM

HARD CANDY

CANDIES

CANDIES

PTA PTA PTA PTA

Music Room 3

DON'T BE SAD, MY LADY. IT WAS PROBABLY BETTER THIS WAY...

MASTER TAMAKI, I'M SO DISAPPOINTED.

I REALLY WANTED YOU TO TASTE THE CUSTOM-MADE CHOCOLATES FROM MY PATISSERIE...

I WISH YOU'D ACCEPT...

NO MATTER HOW ELEGANT THE CHOCOLATE IT WOULD HAVE MELTED AWAY FROM THE PASSION OF OUR LOVE.

MASTER TAMAKI!

WE NEEDN'T HAVE WORRIED ABOUT HIM...

OUR PROMISE NEED NOT BE TANGIBLE!

NATURALLY! HEH. NO MATTER WHAT CIRCUMSTANCE, CUSTOMER SATISFACTION IS OUR TOP PRIORITY!

WHO SAID IT WAS AN ACT?

CLAP

WONDROUS, MILORD. NICE ACT.

YOU'RE QUICK AT SHIFTING GEARS.

HUNNY...

Did I...

Haruhi, am I a bad boy?

...

...do something to offend God?

#3: "PERSUA-SION BY TEARS"

GRAB

...

IT LOOKS A LITTLE LIKE CHOCOLATE. (I MEAN, ITS COLOR.)

HERE.

!!

YOU CAN HAVE JUST A LITTLE, ALL RIGHT?

TUP

MATIMO KELP

HUNNY ASKED THE WRONG PERSON.

AH!!

HARUHI, NO!!

SHHH

USUALLY, MORI ACCEPTS THEIR CHOCO-LATES WARMLY. THAT'S HIS WAY OF REJECTING THEIR LOVE.

MORI IS TOO NICE A GUY...

...TO HURT A GIRL'S FEELINGS.

HE COLDLY REJECTED THAT GIRL TO HURT HER...

...SO IT WOULD HURT HIM EVEN MORE.

STOPPING HUNNY FROM EATING SWEETS, AND NOT PARTICIPATING IN VALENTINE'S DAY...

2

HARUHI FUJIOKA
✿ **BORN ON FEBRUARY 4TH** ✿
⇩

OF ALL THE SUGGESTIONS, THIS DATE RECEIVED THE MOST. YOU JUST CAN'T ARGUE THAT THE FIRST DAY OF SPRING = "HARU". SO, IT WAS A NATURAL CHOICE. I ALSO GOT SUGGESTIONS FOR DATES ASSOCIATED WITH THE CHANGING OF THE SEASONS, FLORAL LANGUAGE, AND SO FORTH. THANK YOU ALL SO MUCH!!

AT THE BEGINNING, HARUHI MEANT "DISTANT SUN" IN KANJI, BUT AFTER FOUR VOLUMES SHE FEELS MORE LIKE THE KANJI FOR "SPRING DAY" TO ME. (IT DOES OVERLAP WITH KANAKO'S LAST NAME FROM THE CHRISTMAS EPISODE, THOUGH.)

BY THE WAY, THE REASON WHY I WRITE "HARUHI" IN KATAKANA IS THAT ALL THE OTHER CLUB MEMBERS HAVE SUCH IMPRESSIVE NAMES THAT MY EDITOR SUGGESTED IT FOR CONTRAST.

THE LAYOUT OF THE FUJIOKA FAMILY HOME IS MODELED AFTER THE PLACE I USED TO LIVE UNTIL JUST RECENTLY. (LAUGH) MY KITCHEN WAS A BIT BIGGER. THE TATAMI ROOM LOOKED PRETTY MUCH THE SAME, THOUGH.

EVEN IF WE CANNOT RETURN THEIR AFFECTION...

...AT LEAST WE CAN OFFER A ROSE.

WHAT?!

WHY?! WHAT ABOUT ME?

I ALSO MADE CHOCOLATE FOR THE CELEBRA-TION.

HERE.

A FEW DAYS LATER

FLO MP!!

DEAR HUNNY

CONGRATU-LATIONS

ONCE HUNNY HAD FULLY RECOVERED, HE RECEIVED A MOUND OF CHOCOLATES FROM HIS CUSTOMERS.

4

KYOYA OHTORI
🌸 **BORN ON
NOVEMBER 22ND.**
🠗 🌸

IT'S ON "GOOD MARRIED COUPLES DAY"... I'M SORRY (LAUGH). MANY OF YOU SUGGESTED NOVEMBER 3RD (CULTURAL DAY) OVER ANY OTHER DATE, BUT SOMEHOW IT DIDN'T FEEL QUITE RIGHT TO ME. BUT I DIDN'T HAVE ANY OTHER DAY THAT I FELT STRONGLY ABOUT EITHER. I FIGURED A BAD JOKE WOULD DO NO HARM, SO I CHOSE THIS DAY (LAUGH). I MEAN, IT'S EASY TO REMEMBER, RIGHT?

KYOYA WAS ALWAYS A SECRET FAVORITE OF SOME FANS, BUT AFTER THE OCEAN EPISODE IN VOLUME 3, HIS POPULARITY JUMPED. I'M GRATEFUL.

BY THE WAY, DID YOU KNOW THE FIRST TIME KYOYA TOOK OFF HIS GLASSES WAS IN THE *LALA* MAGAZINE PREVIEW? (LAUGH) GLASSES OFF, WITHOUT WARNING? I THOUGHT IT WOULD BE UNUSUAL AND INTERESTING. BUT I REGRETTED IT WHEN I HAD TO HAND-COLOR THE IMAGE... ♪♪
I'M AN IDIOT...

I HAVE A FEELING THAT OLDER FEMALE READERS TEND TO FAVOR TAMAKI.

3

TAMAKI SUOH
🌸 **BORN ON
APRIL 8TH.**
🠗 🌸

APRIL 8TH IS THE BIRTHDAY OF BUDDHA, BUT I CHOSE IT ON A WHIM. ACTUALLY, MANY OF YOU SUGGESTED APRIL 1ST OVER ANY OTHER DATE (LAUGH♪). I CAN SEE WHY.

I CHOSE HIS NAME QUICKLY, WITHOUT MUCH THOUGHT. LATER, THOUGH, I LEARNED FROM A LETTER I RECEIVED THAT SUOH MEANS "ONE WHO BECOMES A KING BECAUSE HE IS DESTINED TO." THAT'S PRETTY COOL. ♪ I ACTUALLY LIKE THE NAME "TAMAKI SUOH" A LOT.

HE'S BECOMING MORE AND MORE FOOLISH. FANS OF THE TWINS NEVER DID LIKE HIM, BUT NOW THEY HAVE DECLARED THEIR HATRED FOR HIM OUTRIGHT BY DEMANDING HE CEASE GOING ANYWHERE NEAR HARUHI... ♪♪ HEH. THAT'S PRETTY BAD. HANG IN THERE, TAMAKI!!!

(AS IF IT'S SOMEONE ELSE'S PROBLEM...)

GUEST ROOM: FAXES ①
SPECIAL
THANKS TO MEKA TANAKA!!

Welcome Home, Disco...!!

MEKA

THIS IS A WONDERFULLY FOOLISH LORD. IT'S AWESOME!! I AM SO GLAD I
CONTINUED TO DRAW MANGA WHEN I CAN BEFRIEND PEOPLE WHO PRODUC
WONDERFUL WORKS THAT I RESPECT. (I MEAN, I'M NOT TALKING ABOUT
THIS DRAWING OF TAMAKI.) ABOUT THIS FAX. AFTER I VISITED MEKA WITH
MS. NARI KUSAKAWA, I HAD TO GO HOME AND WORK. WHEN I GOT HOME
WAS FEELING LOW, AND THE TWO OF THEM SENT ME A FAX AS IF THEY HA
TIMED IT PERFECTLY! IT MADE ME CRY WITH JOY! APPARENTLY, DISCO IS
MADE-UP NICKNAME FOR BISCO. DISCO KATORI.

EPISODE 15

GUEST ROOM: FAXES 2

SPECIAL THANKS TO NARI KUSAKAWA!!

I love him!

Welcome home, Hatorine.

EVERYONE, INCLUDING MYSELF, AGREES THAT I AM A HUGE NARI KUSAKAWA FAN. AND THAT'S WHY I COVET EVERYTHING THAT HAS ANYTHING TO DO WITH THE WORK SHE PRODUCES--AND WHY I ALWAYS MAKE A BIG FUSS ABOUT IT. I TRULY LOVE THIS ARTIST. I MEAN IT.

NARI IS A SMALL, CUTE LADY, BUT SOMEHOW THIS SELF-PORTRAIT SEEMS TO RESEMBLE HER VERY WELL. I WONDER WHY...

B-KO

WHENEVER I EAT INSTANT RAMEN,

NARIKO

I USUALLY EAT THIS KIND.

DON-BEI

GREEN

I LOVE THAT OLD-FASHIONED FLAVOR...

Nari Kusakawa drew.

↓ LOOK AT HER ELEGANT SENSE... ↓

※THIS EPISODE PARALLELS *ALICE IN WONDERLAND*.

※ COSTUME FITTING

WHAT? OUT OF IDEAS FOR THE MAIN STORY?

FROM THE LOOK OF THE SPLASH PAGE, I WONDER IF I'M THE CATERPILLAR...

RIGHT ON THE MARK.

HMPH!

TSK TSK

AMATEURS! YOU DON'T GET IT, DO YOU?

THERE ARE ENOUGH CHARACTERS IN *ALICE*. I WAGER SHE THOUGHT IT WAS A SAFE AUTHOR. CHOICE.

OH WELL. AFTER ALL, A LOT OF PEOPLE REQUESTED THIS.

OH!

THAT MEANS, THE MAIN ATTRAC- TION IS...

IT'S ALICE.

CRACKLE

Well, let's start then.

Once upon a time...

WHAT A CUMBER- SOME OUTFIT.

FLOOFLE

HARUHI IN A FRILLY APRON!!

71

Because Alice was hardly ever curious...

...she would never follow a rabbit thoughtlessly.

LET ME SEE, WHERE WAS I?

FOOSH

The Queen will be upset!

☆ THE END ☆

ER...

OH...

THIS IS HOW IT WOULD TURN OUT.

WAIT, RABBIT-FACE!!

So let's continue with the Hitachiin brothers as Alice.

TRUMP TRUMP

THE PERFECT THING TO KILL TIME, EH, ALICE A?

THE PROBLEM IS...

A TALKING RABBIT IS EXTREMELY RARE, IS IT NOT, ALICE B?

HOW DO WE FIT THROUGH THIS TINY DOOR?

TIP TIP TIP

AMAZING. HUNNY CAN SHRINK DOWN AT WILL.

THIS DRINK IS PERFECT AT A TIME LIKE THIS!

THE☆SHRINKER

bb URM

WAS THERE A CHARACTER LIKE THAT IN THE BOOK?

MU HA HA. I'M THE "MYSTERIOUS MERCHANT N."

WHO ARE YOU?

BEYOND THAT DOOR LIES A WORLD OF MAGIC.

IF YOU DRINK THIS, YOU'LL SHRINK IN AN INSTANT...

MU HA HA.

IF YOU TRAVEL UNEQUIPPED, YOU WILL REGRET IT.

SMIRK

...AND IF YOU EAT LA☆EXPANDER, WHICH COMES WITH THE☆ SHRINKER, YOU CAN WONDER-FULLY AND GIGANTICALLY EXPAND.

LET'S BE BOLD...

UMMM.

UNTIL RECENTLY, OUR RICH LAND WAS RULED BY THE RED QUEEN...

...AND WE USED TO LIVE IN PEACE.

BUT AFTER THE QUEEN FELL ILL, THE BLACK QUEEN TOOK OVER AND OUR TROUBLE BEGAN.

THE BLACK QUEEN IS TEMPERA-MENTAL.

A RED QUEEN

A BLACK QUEEN

IF ANYONE UPSETS THE QUEEN A LITTLE, IT LEADS TO AN IMMEDIATE EXECUTION ORDER.

EVEN IF ONE ESCAPES, IT'S IMPOS-SIBLE TO ELUDE THE CURSE...

THIS FOREST DID NOT SATISFY HER SENSE OF BEAUTY, SO SHE CURSED IT BY TAKING AWAY ITS LIGHT.

KAO   HIKA

5

HIKARU & KAORU
HITACHIIN
☆BORN ON
JUNE 9TH☆
⇓
ALTHOUGH JUNE 6TH WAS
THE MOST POPULAR
SUGGESTION, BASED ON
THE IDEA THAT THEY'RE
"AKIN BUT DISTINCT," I
CHOSE THE 9TH. I HOPE
YOU CAN SEE THAT THEIR
DIFFERENCES ARE
SLOWLY BEING REVEALED
IN EACH VOLUME.

☆TRIVIA FOR YOU.☆

THEY ADDRESS
THEMSELVES AS BOKU
BUT OCCASIONALLY,
HIKARU USES ORE.
I WONDER IF ANYONE
HAS NOTICED. ♪

AT THE SUGGESTION OF MY
ASSISTANT, I WATCHED
A TV SHOW CALLED
"OH! MICKEY" AND THERE
I FOUND AN EXCELLENT
SET OF MANIACAL TWINS!
(↑THIS IS A COMPLIMENT!!)
(LAUGH.) THE SHOW HAS
GREAT DIALOG AND IS
EXTREMELY FUNNY.
(I BOUGHT THE DVD
IMMEDIATELY.) WHETHER
YOU LIKE THE TWINS OR
NOT, YOU SHOULD CHECK
IT OUT!!

(THE HERO ISN'T A TWIN!)

Of course, Alice had no interest in fighting the Queen...

...but as she was true of heart, she felt obliged to keep her promise.

OH DEAR! BE CAREFUL!

TMP TMP TMP TMP

I'LL GATHER SOME INFORMATION FIRST.

LET ME HELP YOU!!

ALICE C.

LOOK WHAT TROUBLE I'VE FALLEN INTO, THANKS TO ALICE C.

EXCUSE ME. ABOUT THE BLACK QUEEN...

HMMM. THE QUEEN IS QUITE CRUEL, THEN....

To gather more information, the level-headed Alice...

BUT WHAT DO I DO? I DON'T EVEN KNOW WHERE THE QUEEN IS.

...decided to visit someone known as the "Well-Informed Duchess."

OH!! ARE YOU SAYING...

...THAT YOU'LL DEFEAT THE BLACK QUEEN FOR MY SAKE?!

GLINT GLINT GLINT

DUCHESS = RENGE HOSHAKUJI

...RECEIVED A DEATH SENTENCE FROM THE BLACK QUEEN.

BUTLER

DIS-TRESS?

AND IT'S NOT FOR YOUR SAKE, REALLY...

DEFEAT...? I MEAN, I'LL TALK TO HER...

HUH?

SNFF SNFF

I WAS ONLY...

WHAT DID I DO?

WELL... THE DUCHESS ACTU-ALLY...

OF COURSE! I KNEW IT!

I KNOW!! IT IS THE NATURAL ORDER FOR A HERO TO APPEAR WHEN A DAMSEL IS IN DISTRESS.

OH YES.

YOU BROUGHT IT ON YOURSELF, THEN...

BOO HOO HOO

TACHIBANA

QUEEN

...CURIOUS ABOUT THE BLACK QUEEN AND HER RELATIONSHIP WITH HER ATTENDANT, TACHIBANA...

I ONLY GOSSIPED A LITTLE.

SNIFFLE

IF ANYTHING HAPPENS TO ME, WHAT WILL BECOME OF MY DEAR BABY?

BUT THE LOOKS THEY EXCHANGE SCREAM DEEPER MEANINGS!!

AND HE HAD HIS ARM AROUND HER ONCE!!

OKAY, OKAY.

The Duchess's network of information turned out to be a web of fancies.

MAY I SEE?

IS IT A BOY OR A GIRL?

HUH?

YOU HAVE A BABY?

AH, A GIRL THEN.

ALICE'S REPLY IS INCORRECT.

SUCH A QUIET BABY. NEVER CRIED EVEN ONCE...

EEE!

I NAMED THE BABY MORIKO.

WE'RE HERE TO COLLECT YOU!!

DUCHESS! BY ORDER OF THE BLACK QUEEN....

KA-BLANG!!

MAY RABBIT= WHITE (BORN IN MAY)

A BOGUS HATTER AND A MAY RABBIT!!

HA!

FOOLISH CATS! YOU MAKE ME LAUGH.

DEMANDING THINGS FROM A HELPLESS GIRL. IT'S THE WORST A GENTLEMAN CAN DO.

ROLE #2: HATTER

I THOUGHT YOU WERE EXECUTED LONG AGO.

HE WAS IMPRISONED AFTER HE PER- FORMED SOME ODD STAGE MAGIC DURING A CROQUET GAME SPONSORED BY THE QUEEN.

BOGUS?

HEY!

HEY!

NO WAY.

THAT'S WORSE THAN ASKING FOR MONEY.

I WILL PROTECT YOU AND DEFEAT THE QUEEN IF YOU PROMISE TO MARRY ME.

THE LIFE OF A FUGITIVE IS DIFFICULT, MILADY.

HE4!

BREAKING OUT OF JAIL WAS A PIECE OF CAKE!!

Don't get carried away, fools!

Had the queen not stopped me, I would have finished you in an instant.

DARK MODE RETURNS

HE'S THE RABBIT FROM EARLIER...

HIS APPEARANCE CHANGED DRASTICALLY.

THAT RABBIT HAS A DOUBLE PERSONALITY.

HUSH.

PSST PSST

I BET IT'S BECAUSE WE'RE RUNNING OUT OF PAGES.

HOW DISAP- POINT- ING.

Be quiet, you worms!!

WELL, THAT SURE WAS EASY.

I EX- PECTED SOME ACTION

I despise vermin like you.

GLO OM

TOLD OFF BY A RABBIT...

...ARE CONDUCTED TO BENEFIT THE KINGDOM. PLEASE UNDERSTAND THIS.

EXECU- TIONS AND OTHER PUNISH- MENTS...

YOU SEEM TO MISUNDER- STAND.

ARTIFICIAL

THEY USED LIGHT FROM AN ARTIFICIAL SUN THAT THEY HAD INSTALLED WITH TAXPAYER MONEY.

THE SUN DOESN'T REACH THAT FOREST TO BEGIN WITH.

...IT WAS SIMPLY FOR THE SAKE OF REDUCING THE COST OF UTILITIES.

IN THE CASE OF THE CURSED FOREST OF ROBERIA...

HOW DARE YOU SAY THAT!!

REGARDING THE CHESHIRE CAT'S PUNISHMENT...

EEE! EEE!

THE BLESSING OF THE SUN!

HUH?

ELEPHANT TORTOISE

THE HATTER DESTROYED THE CROQUET GAME...

THE ELEPHANT TORTOISE HE COOKED WAS SUPPOSED TO HAVE BEEN USED FOR BREEDING A NEW NATIONAL FOOD SOURCE.

...WHICH WAS SUPPOSED TO BRING IN A LARGE SUM IN FOREIGN DONATIONS.

AND THE DUCHESS WASTED A HUGE AMOUNT OF PAPER ON GROUNDLESS GOSSIP.

YAY

Secret ♥Love!

IN OTHER WORDS, MAKING DOUJINSHI

THANKS TO THE SPENDTHRIFT RED QUEEN...

YES.

IT SOUNDS AS IF...

WOO

AAH!
AAH!
AAH!

WOOOOOO

And that's how the Black Queen and the castle vanished.

I wonder what happened to me?

6

MITSUKUNI HANINOZUKA
☆*BORN ON
FEBRUARY 29TH.*☆
⇩
BECAUSE HIS BIRTHDAY
COMES ONLY ONCE
EVERY FOUR YEARS,
HE GROWS ONCE EVERY
FOUR YEARS. THAT'S
THE IDEA...

ORIGINALLY, THE PREMISE
FOR HIS CHARACTER
(BEFORE THE FIRST
EPISODE WAS DRAWN) WAS
"HE LOVES FLOWER
GARDENS, BUNNY
RABBITS, AND CAKES. HE
LOVES OLDER WOMEN
JUST AS WELL. HE IS
KNOWN AS THE ONLY BOY
IN THE CLUB WHO CAN BE
VIOLENT TOWARD WOMEN,
ALTHOUGH NO ONE HAS
EVER WITNESSED SUCH A
SCENE. WHEN HE IS
EXTREMELY IRATE, HE WILL
SAY, 'GET LOST, PIGS!'
TO THE LADIES."
THERE WERE MANY SCARY
THINGS WRITTEN ABOUT
HIM IN THERE. HE ALSO
WAS SUPPOSED TO HAVE
A PERFECT DOUBLE
PERSONALITY. TAMAKI'S
SQUATTING POSE, WHICH
HE ASSUMES WHEN
FEELING DEJECTED, WAS
ORIGINALLY PLANNED FOR
HUNNY.

THINGS CHANGE
OVER TIME, INDEED.
SERIOUSLY...

☆HUNNY FROM
THE EARLY
CHARACTER LIST

UMMM.

I'M SO
SLEEPY.

EPISODE 16

SWSH

PRESIDENT!! WE'VE FINALLY HIT 10% CIRCULATION. PLEASE MAKE THE DECISION! IT'LL BE THE KEY TO OUR CONTINUED EXISTENCE.

CALM DOWN, SAKYOU.

UKYOU, DON'T BE RASH. IT'S DANGEROUS TO GET INVOLVED WITH THAT CLUB!

IF WE FAIL, NOT ONLY WILL OUR CLUB BE SHUT DOWN--WE COULD BE EXPELLED...

AS UKYOU POINTED OUT, WE MUSN'T ALLOW OUR CLUB TO BE SHUT DOWN... THEREFORE, WE HAVE NO CHOICE BUT TO BOW DOWN...

NEWSPAPER CLUB

...TO THE HOST CLUB...

A MID-SPRING TALE FROM THE OURAN INSTITUTE

NOTE
PLEASE IGNORE THE FACT
THAT, FOR VARIOUS REASONS,
THEY AGAIN FAIL TO
ADVANCE A GRADE THIS YEAR.

DO YOU REMEMBER WHAT HAPPENS TO YOU, KAORU, WHEN YOU PLAY THE PENALTY GAME ALONE WITH ME?

HMM

WHAT?! WHAT HAPPENS?

EEE! EEE!

BUT, HIKARU, THAT'S...

IN THE HEIAN ERA, PEOPLE USED TO SEE THE FOUR SEASONS BY THE DRIFTING PETALS AND COLORED LEAVES...

WE HAD IT CUSTOM-INSTALLED SO THAT WE MAY ENJOY THE SEASONS WITH YOU LADIES.

THIS IS CALLED YARIMIZU STREAM.

I DIDN'T NOTICE IT BEFORE.

WOW. THERE'S A NICE STREAM IN THE COURT-YARD...

EEE!

PLEASE RESERVE A PLACE FOR ME!!!

RESERVATION BOOK

THAT REMINDS ME....HOW ABOUT A TEA PARTY IN AUTUMN--WITH A LIMITED GUEST LIST?

IT'S A TABLOID THAT EXAGGERATES LOVE AFFAIRS BETWEEN STUDENTS, CLASS DIVISIONS DUE TO FAMILY RIVALRIES, AND SO ON.

THEY PRODUCE ONLY THIS-- THE SO-CALLED "OU SPOT."

THEIR FABRICATIONS HAVE GOTTEN SO WILD THAT NO ONE READS IT ANYMORE.

OH, I DIDN'T KNOW THERE WAS A NEWS-PAPER CLUB.

I DON'T KNOW ANYTHING ABOUT THE OTHER CLUBS.

TEACHER K
ANTI HAIR-LOSS
NOT "BEGINNING" BUT "REPLACING"?

TRAGIC LOVE!!
OU SPOT
CLASS
DIFF RENG

3-A Lady Ak
2-D Mr. Takazaki

DOMESTIC FIGHT
FOOTBALL CLUB
THE RIPPLE EFFECT OF TAKATSUKI'S HEAVY INDUSTRY MERGER

"IN THE FOOT-STEPS OF HOST CLUB: 24-7!!"

PLEASE LEND US YOUR AID!!

SURE... IN OUR QUEST FOR READERSHIP, WE LOST SIGHT OF THE TRUTH.

FOR THE SPRING SPECIAL, WE'D LIKE TO REVEAL THE TRUTH ABOUT YOUR CHARM IN "IN THE FOOT-STEPS OF THE HOST CLUB: 24-7!!"

REALLY?

BUT WITH THE IMMINENT CLOSURE OF OUR CLUB, OUR EYES WERE OPENED.

WE REFUSE!!

BOOM

KRA-

KKA-

WAHHH!
Tamaki!
You okay?

Music Room 3

CRUNCH

CORNIES

...

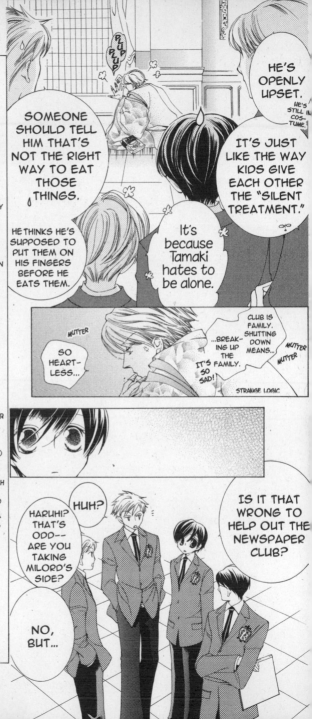

7

TAKASHI MORINOZUKA
BORN ON
✩**MAY 5TH.**
⬇

THIS ONE IS ACTUALLY BASED ON THE MAJORITY VOTE. "CHILDREN'S DAY" FEELS LIKE A MISMATCH, AND THAT'S WHY I LIKE IT. MEANWHILE "BOYS FESTIVAL" IS PERFECT, AND THAT MAKES IT EVEN BETTER.

MORI IS SUPPOSED TO BELONG TO THE KENDO CLUB TOO... BUT HOW COME NO KENDO SCENE HAS APPEARED WHEN WE'RE ALREADY INTO VOLUME 4? I KNOW... I MEANT TO DRAW ONE, BUT PLEASE WAIT A LITTLE WHILE LONGER.

BY THE WAY, MOST LETTERS COME FROM FANS OF EITHER MORI OR THE TWINS--DESPITE THE FACT MORI HARDLY EVER IS PART OF THE ACTION. I'M GRATEFUL. MORI IS BY HIMSELF ON THE OPENING PAGE OF EPISODE 13, EVEN THOUGH HE WAS BARELY IN THE STORY. I JUST WANTED TO TRY SOMETHING MEANINGLESS LIKE THAT. (SELF-SATISFACTION)

IF KYOYA SAYS SO.

WE'LL GO ALONG.

GOT IT, EVERY-ONE?

WE WILL PROVIDE A PLAN FOR THE SPECIAL FEATURE.

WE'LL DO IT UNDER CERTAIN CONDITIONS.

Okay! ♡

CUSTOMERS MUST NOT BE BOTHERED, SO THE SERVICE SCENE IS OUT.

AND THE INTERVIEW IS FORBIDDEN.

YEAH, YEAH.

READY!

LET'S GO!!

HITACHI-INS, ANY IDEAS?

RIGHT!! LET'S START PLANNING NOW!!

NEWSPAPER CLUB

I GUESS WE HAVE NO CHOICE BUT TO ACCEPT THEM.

IS THAT RIGHT? THEY SET DOWN CONDI-TIONS?

AT THE VERY LEAST, WE'VE SUCCEEDED IN ENTERING THE ENEMY'S CAMP.

BUT LOOK...

HEH

HOST CLUB

IT IS A GROUP OF HANDSOME MEN (WITH ONE EXCEPTION) WHO SHOWCASE THEIR SUPREME A-CLASS LINEAGE AND ACADEMIC ACHIEVEMENTS AT OURAN, WHERE THE CHILDREN OF NOBLE FAMILIES GATHER.

IT IS AN UNUSUAL CLUB THAT TAMAKI SUOH, THE CURRENT PRESIDENT, ESTABLISHED WHEN HE ENTERED HIGH SCHOOL.

SHE'S THE EXCEPTION.

IT WAS AN IMMEDIATE SUCCESS AMONG FEMALE STUDENTS.

GENERAL CLUBS

CULTURAL CLUB FEDERATION

ATHLETIC CLUB FEDERATION

HOST CLUB

ORGANIZATIONAL CHART OF OURAN CLUBS

THE FACT THAT IT BELONGS TO NO ATHLETIC OR CULTURAL CATEGORY, AND HAS NO TEACHER ASSIGNED TO IT, HAS SHOCKED MANY STUDENTS.

TAMAKI SUOH MUST HAVE ESTABLISHED THE CLUB TO SHOW OFF HIS POWER TO THE OTHER STUDENTS.

EVEN THOUGH THEY ARE A GROUP OF THE TOP STUDENTS, THEIR ARROGANCE IS NOTHING BUT SUOH'S POWER DISPLAY.

THEY OPENLY CONDUCT LOVE FRAUD AT SCHOOL. THEY ALSO REMODELED THE COURTYARD WITHOUT PERMISSION.

YOU'VE SEEN IT YOUR-SELF.

HE PRETENDS TO BE A NICE AND SWEET IDIOT.

ABOUT HOST CLUB? IT'S A SECRET.

BUT THE STUDENTS HARDLY EVER COMPLAIN.

HA HA HA HA.

SUOH? AH, HIM? HE IS, YOU KNOW...

TAMAKI SUOH... I WAGER HE'S AN EXCEPTIONALLY SHREWD MAN.

FEMALE STUDENTS KEEP THEIR MOUTHS SHUT. MALE STUDENTS WHO KNOW SUOH ARE EVASIVE...

HE'S DEVELOPING AN INCREDIBLE ILLUSION.

WE'LL DEFINITELY GET A GREAT SCOOP--AND WE'LL SHOW THE WHOLE SCHOOL THE REAL POWER OF THE NEWSPA-PER CLUB!!

YES, SIR!!

I'M BETTING HE HAS A DARK SIDE!!

HIS IMAGE

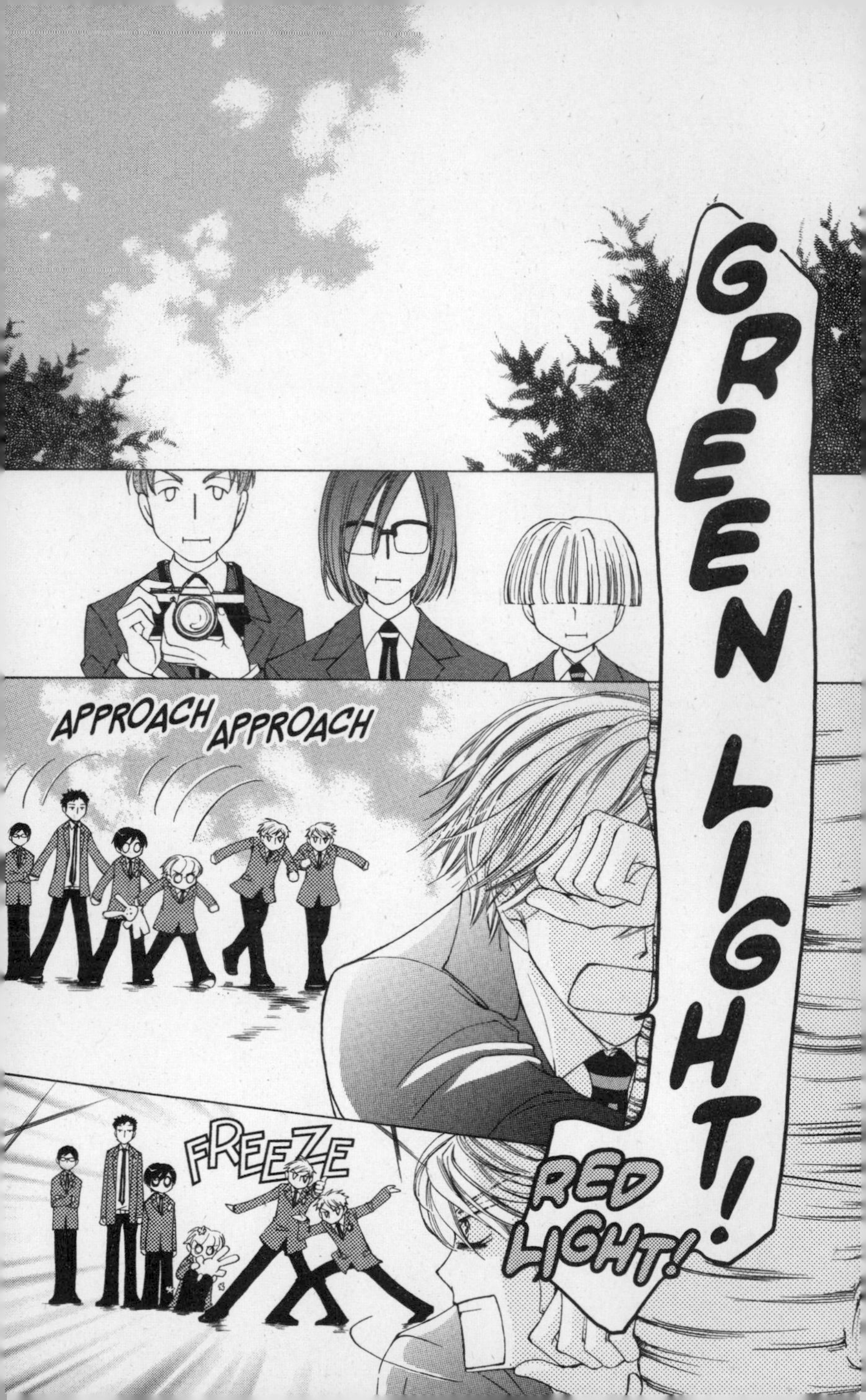
GREEN LIGHT!
APPROACH APPROACH
RED LIGHT!
FREEZE

FRIENDLINESS IS CRITICAL FOR WIPING AWAY THE NEWSPAPER CLUB'S NEGATIVE IMAGE AND GAINING BACK THE READERS!!

ACCORDING TO OUR CALCULATIONS, IT WILL WORK!!

FWASH!

FRIEND-LINESS!!

?!

NEWSPAPER INSIDE TAMAKI'S HEAD

HOST CLUB ENJOYS A COMMONERS GAME

OU SPOT

Lured by Spring!

AN OUTDOOR GAME WILL LET YOU CAPTURE THE IMAGE OF SPRING IN THE BACK-GROUND. IT'S SO ELEGANT-- PERFECT FOR THE FRONT PAGE ARTICLE!!

TO TOP IT OFF, IT WILL MAKE COMMON FOLK VERY HAPPY. IT'S A DREAM EVENT!!

Host Club members savor a typical proletariat diversion

"Thank you, Tamaki!" says Haruhi Fujioka (1-A), of common lineage, and comments that he hasn't had fun like this for a long while. Tamaki Suoh (2-A, King of the Host Club) suggested the event.

On the 24th, the Host Club sponsored an event called "Let's Play Traditional Games of the Common Folk." The Newspaper Club was invited to preview the event...

COMMON FOLK SWEETS 100

"HANDSOME MEN OF HOST CLUB PLAY A COMMON FOLK GAME!!"

PRESIDENT... I DON'T GET IT AT ALL...

HE MIGHT BE NOTHING BUT AN IDIOT...

HE'S LOOKING AT ME...

SHOULD I ACT EXCITED...?

BE QUIET!!

SWIP

HEH

SWIP

HUH? WHERE ARE THE GUYS FROM THE NEWSPAPER CLUB?

THEY CANCELED THE ARTICLE DUE TO SOME EMERGENCY.

OH.

WHAT?!

WHAT WERE YOU DOING WITH HARUHI, MILORD?

SH-SHUT UP!!

SUSPICIOUS.

Ah, Tamaki! Haruhi! I found you!

THEY SAID THEY'LL BE PUBLISHING NORMAL ARTICLES FROM NOW ON.

I BET THEY WON'T HAVE TO SHUT DOWN.

OH...

REALLY?

THAT'S OKAY THEN.

?

BANKING WAS THEIR BASE IN THE OLD DAYS, AND NOW THEIR BUSINESS COVERS MANY FIELDS.

AH...YES. THEY'RE ONE OF THE SEVEN GREAT FAMILIES.

KYOYA, IS THE SUOH FAMILY THAT GREAT?

YAY! CAKE! CAKE!

Let's go back to the clubhouse and have some cake!

YOU'VE NEVER HEARD OF THEM? YOU KNOW, THE LOWA-GRAN HOTEL AND THE OUTO THEATER...

OH, I SEE THOSE ON TV OFTEN.

HMM...

THIS SCHOOL.

AND, OF COURSE, THEY RUN THE SCHOOL.

WHICH SCHOOL?

...

AH... COME TO THINK OF IT, HARUHI...

HUH...

YOU SHOULD AT LEAST REMEMBER THE NAME OF YOUR SCHOOL BOARD CHAIRMAN.

YOU'RE ABLE TO COME TO THIS SCHOOL THROUGH THE SUPPORT OF TAMAKI'S FAMILY.

HUH...

SON OF THE CHAIRMAN

AT THE START OF THE SCHOOL YEAR, HARUHI LEARNED SOMETHING SHE WOULD HAVE BEEN HAPPIER NOT KNOWING.

DOES HARUHI'S FUTURE HANG IN THE BALANCE?!

HUH?!!

OURAN HIGH SCHOOL HOST CLUB, VOL. 4 / THE END

GUEST ROOM: FAXES ③
SPECIAL THANKS TO AKANE OGURA!!

SHE'S ESSENTIALLY MY DRINKING BUDDY, BUT NOWADAYS I'M AUDACIOUS ENOUGH TO HAVE HER HELP ME WITH MY DRAFTS. SHE'S A MEMBER OF LALA'S MANGAKA GROUP.

SHE'S ALSO SOMEONE WHO PRODUCES WONDERFUL WORK. I MEAN, LOOK AT THIS TAMAKI AND HARUHI... SO BEAUTIFUL... (TEARS OF GRATITUDE)

FROM AKANE.

AKANE OGURA AND I

① THE HOST CLUB'S CLIENTS ARE ALL CUTE GIRLS.

WHEN WE WERE DRINKING AT AKANE'S PLACE

REALLY? BUT THEY'RE JUST THE HAPPY-GO-LUCKY SORT OF GIRLS WHO CAN'T GET ENOUGH OF THE HOST CLUB GUYS...

WHAT?

YEAH, THAT'S WHY...

AN AWFUL REMARK.

AKANE IS SUPER GORGEOUS.

② SHE'S...

...SO MATURE!!

TEE HEE...

..THEY'RE SO SILLY AND CUTE LIKE THAT.

I WANNA CALL HER MY BIG SIS!!

BUT IN REALITY, I AM A YEAR OLDER.

LOVE EGOIST

YOU DIOTS!!

OH NO, THAT'S NOT TRUE. ♡

I'M THE NORMAL ONE.

SHE HAS AN EXCEPTIONALLY WICKED PERSONALITY.

RIGHT. THAT'S THE PROB- LEM...

OH NO, I DID IT AGAIN.

CHEMISTRY PREP ROOM

IT'S NOT LIKE I WANTED MY PERSONALITY TO BE THIS WAY.

BUT WHEN THEY GO WILD OVER A SINGLE SMILE, SAYING I'M AN ANGEL OR A GOD- DESS...

AT LEAST SHE'S AWARE OF HER DEFICIENCY.

MY IDOL, MR. SAGINUMA (AGE 25)...

PEOPLE ARE SUCH SIMPLE- TONS.

AH HA HA HA HA

...HOW CAN I HELP BUT RIDICULE THEM?!!

IS A SWEET TEACHER WHO CARES ABOUT HIS STUDENTS AND THEIR EDUCATION.

CHEMISTRY TEACHER

MY SWEET- NESS IS FAKE.

EVEN A LOVE OF THE CENTURY WOULD BE CHILLED BY THAT.

AHH

HE'S HORRIBLE!

OH.

THANKS.

CHATTER CHATTER

I COLLECTED THE NOTES YOU ASKED FOR.

ALL RIGHT. I'LL TAKE ON THE CHALLENGE!

I'M SORRY TO ASK A STUDENT *LIKE YOU* TO TAKE CARE OF A CHORE LIKE THIS.

PLEASE DON'T BE. ♡

I AM HONORED TO BE OF HELP TO A *WONDERFUL* TEACHER LIKE YOU. ♡

ASSIGNED YOU THE WRONG ROLE, DIDN'T I?

IF YOU KNEW IT, YOU SHOULDN'T HAVE ASKED ME.

GRIN

GRIN

YOU TRICKSTER WITH A GENIAL SMILE.

YOU STOMPED ON A MAIDEN'S PURE HEART. AND MY GRUDGE...

TEACHERS ROOM

NOK NOK

MR. SAGINUMA.

HEH.

HEH HEH HEH HEH HEH

...WON'T JUST DISAPPEAR!!

KRAK-KA-BOOM

IT'S A WONDERFUL SIGHT.

BOTH ARE ALSO POPULAR AMONG TEACHERS.

HE'S SO POPULAR AMONG STUDENTS. I ENVY HIM.

YES MR. SAGINUMA? ♡

WOW, IT'S MR. SAGI-NUMA!

SUMIRE, CAN I ASK YOU SOME-THING?

THAT JERK IS TOYING WITH ME!

AND THIS GOES TO THE TEACHERS ROOM, AND THAT—

TUNG!!

TAKE THIS AND THAT TO THE REFERENCE ROOM.

IT'S HEAVY.

PANT

← BECAUSE HE KNOWS HER WEAKNESS, SHE CAN'T REFUSE.

MR. SAGINUMA, EVERYONE AT THE CLASS WAS...

OH NO.

YOU KNOW...

I'M SO PLEASED TO TEACH A SWEET AND INNOCENT STUDENT LIKE YOU.

...TOUCHED BY YOUR WORDS.

BELIEVE YOU WERE TALKING ABOUT HUMAN ETHICS, RIGHT?

YOU'VE GOT NO RIGHT TO THINK THAT.

IF ONLY EVERYONE ELSE WERE JUST LIKE YOU.

IT'S A HUNDRED YEARS TOO SOON FOR YOU TO CRUSH ME. HA.

WSS

2 C

HE'S GOING OVER THE EXAM PAPERS.

WSS

WOW.

THERE'S SOME HUMANITY LEFT IN HIM...

240 YEN, PLEASE.

IT'S YOUR TREAT.

PAY UP!

WSS

IS HE PAYING ATTENTION IN CLASS?

WHAT A NASTY SCORE.

WSS

MR. SAGINUMA...

SIP

← SHE ENDED UP TREATING HIM.

ABSO-LUTELY NOT.

NEVER.

DON'T YOU EVER HATE YOUR PERSON-ALITY?

WHEN DID YOU BECOME LIKE THIS?

I AM A PERFECT MAN, AFTER ALL.

OKAY, I GOT IT.

I DON'T KNOW.

I GUESS I WAS BORN THIS WAY.

I HATE MYSELF SOME-TIMES.

BUT I...

AT FIRST, I WAS SIMPLY FIGHTING THE IMAGE OTHERS FORCED ON ME.

IT'S TRUE THAT IT'S KIND OF FUN TO CURSE PEOPLE BEHIND THEIR BACKS, BUT...

I KNOW IT'S NOT NICE, AND...

IT MAKES ME FEEL DEPRESSED AFTERWARD.

WSS

WSS

IS HE LISTENING, EVEN?

HMPH. IS THAT SO?

I DON'T THINK IT'S AS COMPLEX AS YOU MAKE IT OUT TO BE.

SHIK

FINE. I'M GOING HOME.

...

INSTEAD OF WASTING TIME WORRYING ABOUT IT, WHY DON'T YOU CUT TO THE CHASE AND LOVE YOURSELF?

BESIDES...

WE CAN NEVER ESCAPE WHO WE ARE.

I CAN'T ARGUE WITH THAT KIND OF BOLD STATEMENT.

AND NO TEACHER WOULD MAKE A STUDENT PAY.

HMPH.

AH HA HA HA HA HA HA

HMMM

AND WHERE DOES THAT CONFIDENCE COME FROM?

AHH, HE'S TOO FUNNY.

TEE HEE HEE

THAT'S SO LIKE HIM.

WHY DON'T YOU CUT TO THE CHASE AND LOVE YOUR-SELF?

GLOOOM

I'VE GOT TO WATCH IT.

IT'S AS IF I'VE ACCEPTED HIS PERSONALITY....

OH, SUMIRE?

I WAS IN THE CHEMISTRY ROOM.

CLASSMATE

CHEMIS-TRY...?

SMILE

WHAT'S UP? YOU'RE STILL HERE THIS LATE?

I JUST GOT BACK FROM CLUB.

HI, SAEKI.

AHH...

MR. SAGINU-MA?

SUMIRE.

YOU SAID YOU'D WANT TO CHANGE FOR SOMEONE YOU CARE ABOUT.

LET ME TELL YOU THIS. I'M NOT INTERESTED IN A WOMAN WHO LACKS CONFIDENCE IN HERSELF.

SO...

THERE.

HUH.

WORK HARD!

WHY CAN'T HE JUST SAY HE LIKES HER THE WAY SHE IS?

I AGREE.

BUT...

BE HONEST ALREADY.

OURAN SUSPENSE THEATER

BY
HATORIKOFF
BISCOVITCH

People sometimes imagine a worst-case scenario to find relief in reality.

※ IT'S SIMPLY A "WHAT IF" THEATER.

Case 1: What if Kyoya and Tamaki were swapped inside?

SSS...

...

POTATO RINGS

Crunchy ☆ Potatoes

CHEEN

KYOYA... I MEAN, MILORD, WHAT'RE YOU DOING?

WHETHER OR NOT I CAN ADD ANOTHER POTATO RING-- THE RING-SHAPED SNACK OF THE COMMON FOLK--WILL DETERMINE MY TRUE WORTH AS A MAN...

FOR GUINESS

QUIET! RIGHT NOW I'M CHALLENGING A WORLD RECORD.

HUSH!!

POTATO RING

AAHHH

GACK!

PAKKA PAKKI PATA

TUNK!!

KYOYA INSIDE

HE FEELS UNCOMFORTABLE WITHOUT GLASSES.

WHAT GETS DETERMINED IS THE LENGTH AND THINNESS OF MY FINGERS. THAT'S ALL.

WILL YOU STOP SALTING MY FINGERS FOR A STUPID CHALLENGE, TAMAKI?

BESIDES, WHY ARE YOU SO UNCONCERNED WHEN I'M DESPERATELY RESEARCHING WHY WE CHANGED BODIES?

OH!! HE'S A SMART BUT WICKED SORT OF LORD!!

SORRY ABOUT THE NAUSEATING SCENARIO.

KYOYA...

DON'T WORRY, TAMAKI.

AND OF COURSE, I WILL DO AS MUCH AS I CAN AS TAMAKI SUOH. IT GOES WITHOUT SAYING.

WHILE WE'RE SWAPPED, I'LL STAND BY YOU AND HELP YOU ACT LIKE ME.

↰ IN OTHER WORDS, HE WILL PROVIDE SPARTAN TRAINING.

IT WILL BE A WASTE IF I DON'T EFFECTIVELY USE HIS POWERS AS THE SCHOOL BOARD CHAIRMAN'S SON AND THE KING OF THE HOST CLUB.

SMILE ♡

!!

| Conclusion |
| A man in a position of supreme power is likable when he's a bit of an idiot. Kyoya is better suited as a vice president. |

NOOOOO!

WAHH

GOVERNED BY TERROR
(Too terrible to show)

BOOM

KRAKKA-OM

WOBBLE

...I CAN STILL CARRY HIM.

MORI'S STANDARD FOR JUDGING WEIGHT

IMPOSSIBLE TO LIFT ←→ POSSIBLE TO LIFT
HEAVY   LIGHT

SO WHAT?

GLOOOM

I CAN.

Even if you're overweight, I want you to grow up to be strong.

GLOOOM

THAT WAS SCARY...

A NIGHTMARE...

JOLT

Whether Mori actually thought that is unknown.

Hunny will never gain weight since no one appreciates him that way.

THE END

HEH HEH HEH

AH HA HA HA

I DON'T WANT TO DRAW HIM THAT WAY EVER AGAIN EITHER.

EGOISTIC CLUB

THINKING IT WOULD BE FUN, I DREW OURAN SUSPENSE THEATER. BUT KYOYA IS UNEXPECTEDLY SO NOT CUTE WITH TAMAKI INSIDE. I THOUGHT THAT WAS THE BEST SUSPENSE OF ALL.

HELLO!! THIS IS HATORI.

HATORI'S NEW PET-- A STUFFED ANIMAL. I STICK MY HAND IN ITS MOUTH AND IT HEALS ME. MY FRIEND, MIDORI SHIINO, GAVE IT TO ME.

IT'S COMFORT-ING...

AH...

DEJECTED KYOYA WAS MEANT TO BE COMIC RELIEF, BUT IT TURNED OUT WITH AN UNEXPECTED RESULT.

A BIT OVER 5MM.

IT WAS ABOUT FIVE MILLIMETERS IN LENGTH-- A THIN OBJECT MADE OF PLASTIC OR RUBBER.

WHAT IS THIS?

FOR INSTANCE, WHEN I WAS STILL LIVING IN MY OLD APARTMENT...

HM?

THERE IS PLENTY OF SUSPENSE IN HATORI'S DAILY LIFE TOO.

AND THE FRIGHTENING THING WAS, NO MATTER HOW I CLEANED THEM OFF THE FLOOR, EACH DAY I FOUND THEM SCATTERED EVERYWHERE!!

WHERE DID IT COME FROM? OH, THERE ARE MORE TOO...

IT DIDN'T FALL FROM THE CEILING OR THE WALL...

SEVERAL DAYS PASSED WITHOUT KNOWING THE CAUSE...

OH, MY SLIPPER...

POOT

SUPER TALENTED STAFF, YUI-SAN

I'M SCARED. WHAT DO YOU THINK IT IS, YUI-SAN?

HMMM. SO-CALLED PARANORMAL PHENOMENA, HUH?

NO!! NOT THAT!!

I WONDER WHAT IT IS...

GYAHHH!

← MY FAVORITE HEALTH SANDAL.

...

THERE WERE TONS OF MARKS SHOWING WHERE THE BUMPS HAD CAME OFF IN SWARMS.

IT WAS A FRIGHTENING EXPERIENCE THAT STILL MAKES ME SHIVER NEEDLESSLY.

IT WAS TRULY USELESS.

I MEAN, YOU SHOULD'VE KNOWN THAT AFTER WEARING THEM!!

HUH?! IT'S FROM THAT?!

YUI-SAN...

I'M SORRY. I FIGURED IT OUT...

THAT SUMMER, I LEARNED ANOTHER PIECE OF TRIVIA: THE BUMPS WILL EVENTUALLY COME OFF OF HEALTH SANDALS.

NOW ANOTHER STORY!! LALA MAGAZINE HAD VARIOUS PLANS FOR THE HOST CLUB!!

THANK YOU SO MUCH FOR SENDING YOUR SUBMISSIONS FOR HARUHI'S DRESS DESIGN AND BIRTHDAY!!

THANK YOU SO MUCH!!

yay! ♥

WE'LL STILL USE THE DESIGNS THAT WERE NOT SELECTED FOR OUR FUTURE REFERENCE!!

THE HEIAN COSPLAY IN VOLUME 4 WAS, IN FACT, REQUESTED THE MOST. ☆

LIKE MIKO-STYLE DESIGNS.

FOR THE DRESS DESIGN, THERE WERE MORE TRADITIONAL JAPANESE-STYLE DESIGNS, WHICH IS INTERESTING.

I WONDER IF EVERYONE SIMPLY LOVES THE CLASSIC JAPANESE STYLE?

DUN

VOICE ACTING SUBMISSIONS FOR PRODUC- TION OF THE ZEN-IN DRAMA CD!!

ONLY TWO ARE TO BE SELECTED FROM THEM ALL. IT'S TOO CRAZY.

BUNNY BOX
BUNNY BOX BUNNY BOX
BUNNY BOX BUNNY BOX BUNNY BOX

I'VE HEARD WE RECEIVED SEVEN OR EIGHT BOXES FULL OF SUBMISSIONS.

BUT WHAT SHOCKED ME THE MOST WAS THIS!!

DUN

PLEASE WAIT VERY, VERY, VERY PATIENTLY.

"I'M LOOKING FORWARD TO IT!"

"YOU'RE AMAZ- ING!"

"IT'S INCREDIBLE THAT YOU'LL BE RESPONDING TO MY LETTER!!"

AHHHH. I'M SORRY.

ALSO, I'VE BEEN SAYING I'LL REPLY TO EACH LETTER...

I'M SO SORRY. I HAVEN'T DONE ANY YET!!

Special Thanks!!

THIS TIME I'M TAKING A BREAK FROM THE FLIRTATIOUS DRAWING AT THE END OF THE VOLUME. I'M SUPER-DUPER SORRY!! VOLUME 5 WILL HAVE MORI AND HARUHI!!

THIS IS A REJECTED VERSION OF THE ROUGH DRAWING FOR THE COLOR OPENING PAGE IN EPISODE 2. IT DIDN'T MAKE IT BECAUSE IT LOOKED TOO MUCH LIKE AN IMAGE ILLUSTRATION. DARN IT!! (LAUGH)

✿ THANK YOU TO YAMASHITA, ALL THE EDITORS, AND EVERYONE INVOLVED IN
✿ PUBLISHING THIS BOOK: YUI NATSUKI, AI SATAKE, AYA AOMURA, AKANE OGURA, YUUKI OKANO, RINA HASEGAWA, AND TO YOU, THE READERS. ✿✿

EGOISTIC CLUB / THE END

EDITOR'S NOTES

EPISODE 13

Page 5: The term used in this scene is *oshitaoshi*, a frontal push-down in sumo wrestling.

Page 11: A *genjina* is an alias that nightclub workers use on the job to avoid revealing their true identity. The kanji for *ran* is the same in *Ranka* and *Ouran*. *Ran* means orchid.

Page 21: A *kotatsu* is a low table with a heater underneath.

Page 22: A censored version of the word *Johnnies* was used here, signifying the slang term for pop stars in Japan. It refers to a talent agency known for its boy bands (such as SMAP).

EPISODE 14

Page 45: *Giri* means "obligation." In Japan, women also give *giri choco* (obligation chocolate) on Valentine's Day to their bosses or male friends to show gratitude, not love.

EPISODE 15

Page 83: *Boku* and *ore* are terms that men use to refer to themselves. *Ore* is considered to be coarser (and more dominant) than *boku*.

Page 94: *Doujinshi* is self-published manga, usually made by fans of a particular series.

EPISODE 16

Page 104: The Heian period (784–1185) is known for cultural and artistic achievements. *Heian* means "peace."

Page 109: Hikaru Genji is the main character in *The Tale of Genji*, a novel written in the Heian period about a handsome man and his love affairs at court.

EGOISTIC CLUB

Page 184: A *miko* is a priestess who assists at a shrine. The traditional miko attire is a white shirt with flowing sleeves and a red *hakama*, which looks like a long, wrapped skirt.

LETTERS INTRO ♪

We received a bunch of entries for the April '04 *LaLa* contest "What Should Haruhi Wear?" Many of the designs were really wonderful. Thank you so much!!

We already showed the submissions in *LaLa*, but since we got so many, we're including some in this book too!!

(Kyoya) I say you came up with a splendid idea in covering the chest with frills.

(O, Hirohisma)

(Tamaki) A bubbly Haruhi is also adorable.

(K, Shimane)

Note the big, wavy sash!

The front is rather simple!!

← Blue or pink, for the skirt and ribbon— wouldn't that be darling? 💕

< Back >

How about high heels?

<Feet>

(S, Miyagi)

Tamaki Award

(Tamaki) S-Someone
Fetch the tailor! Get
on this dress, quick!
(Hikaru & Kaoru) M
has picked his favorit

(Mori) I'll escort her...

Haruhi as My Fair Lady ✳

The concept for this design is from the movie "My Fair Lady." I suppose Mori would make a perfect partner, wouldn't he?

+ side +

+ front +

The skirt is wrapped around from behind, and is long enough to hide the shoes.

(M, Saitama)

(Hikaru & Kaoru) Can we get everyone in Host Club to wear this?

PUNK

Fashion.

I chose a punker outfit, knowing Haruhi would never wear it.

The overall color is red. Pink knee-highs. 💕

Brown, thick-soled shoes. (It'd be great if other club members could also wear this.)

(M, Miyagi)

Kyoya Award

(Kyoya) This outfit might boost the Club's profits.
(Tamaki) You are quite the strategist...

(K, Chiba)

(Nara & Aya, Gifu)

(Hikaru & Kaoru) Aim for the Japanese ideal!

(A, Shiga)

(Mori) Cool.

(Tamaki) Behind her—is that...us?

(S, Hyogo)

HARUHI

Since she's tying her hair a bit...

EAST AND WEST MIXED UP FLAVOR DRESS

Use an obi sash for the waist→ It's cute. ∞

Translucent material comes over still woolly black fabric.

A kimono, perhaps? But it's wrapped in soft, wavy, fluttery fabric... Western style. It's a mixture of East and West. Tama-chan may wind up with a bloody nose, huh? →

Note the soft fabric!

← Nose the soft fabric!

← Translucent material.

(Y. Iwate)

→ (Hikaru & Kaoru) Is the theme here gossamer?

(Y. Miyagi)

CHINESE STYLE

What do you think? ☺ I only used shades of pink. Sometimes a miniskirt isn't that bad, eh? I'd love to see Bisco Sensei's version! Will you draw it? ♡

← (Kyoya) A pink Chinese dress... How fresh!

(Tamaki) Gorgeous!

Hikaru & Kaoru Award Award

(Hikaru)
Awesome! The details are thoroughly worked out!
(Kaoru)
It's a classy design.

Chinese-Style Party Dress

The dress looks like this under the jacket. It's made of either satin or cotton.

Soft material

Chinese-Style Jacket

Design for the back.

The bottom part looks like the wings of an angel.

Silver Shoes

(O, Gifu)

(M, Saitama)

Chinese-Style Mermaid Dress

(Hunny) She'll surely look great in it!

(K, Kagawa)

Head

Hand. Light pink

Front

White
Light pink
White

I have a feeling Haruhi would like something simple...

Back

Lace

Haruhi's Wedding Dress

(Hikaru & Kaoru) The veil on her head is nifty.

(I, Gifu)

Were she to work for a pediatrician, she'd attach character pins here.

The pen is a necessity.

HARUHI nurse

Frequently-used items are shoved into the belt.

Shirt long enough to cover the knees.

I tried to retain her youthfulness. I lowered the heels to make it easier to walk around. And I also gave her a pen and scissors. But I left her shirt long enough to cover her knees, to keep Tamaki from freaking out.

Flat heels make walking easier.

(Kyoya) It looks functional and good.

Hunny Award

(Hunny) Yay! Haruhi as a bunny rabbit! (Mori)...

→HARUHI

Hunny's Bun-Bun

♥

(M, Hokkaido)

"WESTERN BOARD GAME DRESS"

black

white white

(H, Saga)

Mori Award

(Mori) ... (So cute)...
(Hunny) Hm?
Takashi, did you say
something?

(K, Gifu)

It's like a dress
from the Exorcist!
(Laugh) With her
rosary and holy
water she's fully
equipped to get rid
of demons!
She might qualify
to become
Nekozawa's
follower...

Demons,
I call
you forth!!
(Laugh)

(T, Okinawa)

(Tamaki) Please
be my bride!

(T, Shimane)

(Kyoya) It's an
Arabian style.

(Hunny) She looks strong!

Thank you for all your entries!

Author Bio

Bisco Hatori made her manga
debut with **Isshun kan no
Romance (A Moment of
Romance)** in **LaLa DX**
magazine. The comedy **Ouran
High School Host Club** is her
breakout hit. When she's stuck
thinking up characters' names,
she gets inspired by loud,
upbeat music (her radio is set
to NACK5 FM). She enjoys
reading all kinds of manga, but
she's especially fond of the sci-fi
drama **Please Save My Earth**
and **Slam Dunk**, a basketball
classic.

OURAN HIGH SCHOOL HOST CLUB
Vol. 4
The Shojo Beat Manga Edition

STORY AND ART BY BISCO HATORI

Translation & English Adaptation/Naomi Kokubo & Eric-Jon Rössel Waugh
Touch-up Art & Lettering/George Caltsoudas
Graphic Design/Izumi Evers
Editor/Nancy Thistlethwaite

Managing Editor/Megan Bates
Editorial Director/Elizabeth Kawasaki
VP & Editor in Chief/Yumi Hoashi
Sr. Director of Acquisitions/Rika Inouye
Sr. VP of Marketing/Liza Coppola
Exec. VP of Sales & Marketing/John Easum
Publisher/Hyoe Narita

Printed in Canada.

Published by VIZ Media, LLC
P.O. Box 77010
San Francisco, CA 94107

Shojo Beat Manga Edition
10 9 8 7 6 5 4 3 2
First printing, December 2005
Second printing, October 2006

Tell us what you think about Shojo Beat Manga!

Our survey is now available online. Go to:

shojobeat.com/mangasurvey

Help us make our product offerings better!